THE

SOUTHERN NEGRO AS HE IS.

BY

G. R. S.,

BOSTON.

"For many are deceived by their own vain opinion; and an evil suspicion hath overthrown their judgment." —*Apocrypha.*

BOSTON:
PRESS OF GEORGE H. ELLIS.
1877.

THE SOUTHERN NEGRO AS HE IS.

THE radical change in the policy of the Republican party towards the South, under the present administration, increases and intensifies the interest of every thoughtful man in the great social problem of the Negro. He is curious about his past, inquisitive as to his present condition, and anxious for his future.

His curiosity and inquisitiveness are easily satisfied, but in them he finds little solace for his anxiety; and the more diligent his research, the more do his solicitude and perplexity increase. In short, the future of the Negro is enigmatic and obscure, and certain facts being known (which only those can know who have associated with him in childhood, and guided him in maturer years), it then can only be indistinctly suggested.

It is a great and prevailing mistake to suppose that the Negro is easily understood, or as readily classified as an ordinary specimen in an anatomical museum. Exact knowledge of him is not acquired by the ordinary traveller in a flying trip to the South, nor, indeed, in a six months' or six years' residence there; on the contrary, nothing but an experience gained by constant intercourse in the field, workshop, and household, can furnish the proper data for a correct opinion of his present status.

A gentleman of culture, who has devoted much study and thought to the subject of the Negro character, says: "Even we who have lived our whole lives among them, are *strangers* to their inner life. Yet those whose opportunities bear no comparison to ours, have more confidence in their opinion than we have, knowing, as we do by experience, the wide difference which interferes with our mutual understanding." "In regard to our views of the Negro, they are at least very friendly to him. I think he has behaved *remarkably well*, and I wish the race the highest success it can attain in the future."

Unfortunately for ourselves and the Negro, we "small philosophers of Massachusetts" have formed our estimate of him as a social element from certain preconceived and indistinct notions, rather than from experience and well-established facts; in many instances yielding up reason to our sympathies. It is our object, so far as it is possible within moderate limits, to present in a cursory way some leading *facts* as to the present condition of the Southern Negro, morally, socially, and politically. An able correspondent of one of our liberal papers in Boston says:—

"By the proclamation of President Lincoln, in 1863, upwards of four million of slaves were suddenly made free, and shortly after, nearly one million were clothed with the rights, privileges, and responsibilities of American citizenship. These acts, so meritorious in themselves, added at once to the already diluted and degraded suffrage of the country an ignorant mass of voters, numbering about one-seventh of the then voting population of the States. A more ignorant and degraded class of people could hardly have been found. Held in bondage for considerably more than a century, after being drawn from a barbarous condition in Africa, they were allowed, and even encouraged, to grow up without education, without morality, and with scarcely more than animal instincts. Naturally they are a kindly people, and their quickness at imitating and copying what comes in their way helps them to acquire, in many instances, gentle ways and habits. Some of them have doubtless been helped by kind masters and mistresses, and by association with white people, and not infrequently by their aptness for simple kinds of music, and for a comforting but superstitious religion. It has been their misfortune, a cruel wrong inflicted upon the race, and not any fault of their own, that they have learned so little. Pages and volumes may be written to recount the wrongs they have suffered. We are not blaming them; we are not apologizing for them; we simply try to look at the actual facts as they exist.

"What sort of a person *is* the average colored voter in the South? We have nothing to do with the creations of fiction, with the prose of Harriet Beecher Stowe, or the poetry of Whittier. Nor in our judgment of the whole race must we be misled by such men as Frederick Douglass, or Joshua B. Smith, or James Wormley, or Revels, or Lynch.

"Of the million of colored voters, more or less, by far the larger portion were known as 'field hands,' ignorant, degraded, licentious, and improvident. In the cities there were exceptions among the mulattoes and quadroons. Some body servants and house servants were exceptionally bright, and exceptionally fortunate in opportunities for improving themselves. But the great mass of colored people in the South are as unfitted to care for themselves, much less to intelligently exercise the suffrage, as can possibly be imagined. Their condition is well-nigh hopeless. They are simply animals. Let us not deceive ourselves, lest by any chance we do them a great and irreparable wrong. I have myself seen colored *statesmen* in the South who could hardly turn their hands or their feeble minds to any labor, even the unexacting one of polishing their own boots. I can testify from observation that the intelligent colored waiters one sees at Saratoga, or Newport, or Sharon Springs, and the quick-witted copper-colored followers of the art tonsorial in our Northern cities, are as far advanced in intelligence and manliness over the most of their Southern brethren as day is brighter than the night. In America every man who stands erect on two legs is a citizen, and however humble he may be, has his rights, which are sacred. Secure to the Negro all his rights by impregnable bulwarks; but for his sake, as well as the larger interests of the country, let us not forget that in most cases he is a child in knowledge, and an animal in instincts and habits.

"When we dismiss from our minds all sentiment and fancy, and all the overdrawn pictures of eloquent oratory and tender poetry, and look at the Southern Negro voter as he is, and apply to his case the principles of statesmanship rather than the vaporings of heated imagination, we shall find him a perplexing study, that will puzzle the largest-hearted and the wisest."

Some time since, we prepared a series of questions under the three heads previously mentioned, which several prominent gentlemen of abundant experience and culture have kindly answered; and we give the answers *verbatim* with an occasional explanatory comment or addition of our own, suggested by inquiry and observation, as presenting, in the most concise, forcible, and practical way, the Negro as he appears in the light of ripe experience, constant observation, and accurate knowledge, to those who are always in contact with him, and are most deeply and personally interested in his present condition and future development.

THE NEGRO MORALLY.

1st. *In what degree do the emotions distinctive of vice and virtue exist as principles of action?*

"The Negro is naturally emotional; he is naturally religious, but his religion is almost entirely sentimental and emotional; he has very little active sense of virtue and vice *as such*, or as principles of action. The *love* of virtue and hatred of vice have little hold on him. When tempted, he generally considers the *immediate consequences* of his action, rather than the question of *right* or *wrong*, and is decided by the seeming probabilities of the case."

2d. *In what degree do the emotions of love and hate exist?* (Involving conjugal, parental, and filial love, resentment and revenge.)

"The conjugal tie is exceedingly weak, and conjugal fidelity generally disregarded. The parental and filial emotions are also very feeble. To his *own* children he is disposed to be overbearing and cruel; to those of the *whites* kind and attentive."

Sir John Lubbock, on marriage and relationships among the lower races of men, says:—

"Marriage and the relationships of a child to its father and mother, seem to us so natural and obvious, that we are apt to look on them as aboriginal and general to the human race. This, however, is very far from being the case. The lowest races have no institution of marriage; true love is almost unknown among them, and marriage in its lowest phases is by no means a matter of affection and companionship."* Resentment and revenge are not *characteristics* of the Negro;

* "Origin of Civilization and Primitive Condition of Man."

he harbors no malice, but his resentment is frequently aroused, and if not at once gratified, soon passes away.

3d. *Has he an accurate conception of his negative duties to others?* (Relating to the taking of life, property, and virtue.)

"When he takes life, it is usually under the *sudden impulse* of passion stimulated by drink, and seldom from revenge, or as a deliberate and planned act. As to property, he has very little perception of *meum et tuum*; it is hard to induce him to believe that stealing, particularly of small things, is a *sin.* Sensuality is the besetting sin of the Negro in both sexes. He has little idea of the restraints of the marriage tie, divorcing himself without the aid of courts, and taking another wife in some distant place, defying identification."

4th. *Has he an accurate conception of the positive duties arising from friendship, and from benefits received?* (Involving gratitude, justice, and mercy.)

"His sense of friendship, gratitude, justice, and mercy is small,—large professions, small performance. There are, however, instances of the very strongest devotion to his benefactors."

5th. *Has he an accurate conception of the positive duties arising from contracts and citizenship?* (Involving the relation of personal service, and patriotic and civic duties.)

"A contract binds him only so long as he thinks it for his advantage. He does not scruple to evade or violate it, because he attaches no sanctity to his promise.

"It is scarcely to be expected that he could, in so short a time since his emancipation, understand much, if anything, of the nature and obligations of citizenship. The future may produce a change, with the change in his political status."

6th. *Has he an accurate conception of his duty to the Deity?* (Involving the character of their worship, and their lives as members of the visible Church.)

"He is *intensely* emotional and superstitious. Religion in some form seems almost a *necessity* to him, and many of the sentimentally religious do seem to have some conception of their relations to the Deity; but there is a vast amount of the *feticism* of their ancestors in Africa, and of modern paganism about them. As to a clear and correct conception of the nature, attributes, and offices of the Holy Trinity, it is rare among the Negro people. In the duties of practical religion they are very deficient."

Sir John Lubbock, in his chapter on the "Character of Religion among the Lower Races of Men," says: "In fact, the so-called religion of the lower races bears somewhat the same relation to religion in its higher forms that astrology does to astronomy, or alchemy to chemistry. Astronomy is derived from astrology, yet their spirit is in entire opposition; and we shall find the same difference between the religions of backward and of advanced races."

We will add that the average Negro is a firm believer in sorcery, enchantments, charms, and the ordinary practices of witchcraft; his worship consists of vehement, impassioned, ecstatic prayer and exhortation; profuse psalm singing (frequently absurdly improvised), the whole often culminating in the "*holy dance*" or "*walk in Egypt*," a relic of African barbarism, in which the contortions of the body furnish a safety-valve to the intense mental excitement. The dawn of day, and absolute nervous and physical exhaustion, call them back to labor and refreshment, frequently prefaced by a walk of several miles to their miserable and cheerless cabins.

In the cities, among the "fashionable" negroes, who closely imitate the whites, the "*holy dance*" is dying out, and is rather looked down upon; but on the plantations it is still kept up.

The ceremonial of baptism is peculiar, and consists of preliminary services in the church; a procession is then formed, headed by the pastor, who is followed by the converts, all in emblematic white robes and white cotton gloves, the congregation bringing up the rear, singing psalms and hymns and spiritual songs, through the streets of the town to the bank of the river. There, after prayer, exhortation, and more singing, they are dipped in the muddy water, and struggle out through the yellow, slimy mud, shouting, in religious frenzy, "Glory to God!" In the afternoon all again repair to the church, the converts dressed in *ball costume* and bridal array, to hear more preaching, and join in congratulations and singing. This is kept up until evening, with gradually increasing fervor, until the climax of the holy dance.

Petty thieving in the ordinary Negro mind does not conflict with his good and regular standing in the church; in fact, small thefts are not considered sins; or, as an old Negro woman expressed it when reproved for robbing the turkey-roost and then presenting herself at the communion-table, "*Do you suppose I would allow a miserable turkey gobbler to stand between me and my blessed Saviour?*"

We were much surprised to find the *black* church membership in Georgia so much smaller than the *white*, but do not know if the proportion is the same in the other cotton States. We, however, give below the membership in Georgia:

The Baptists have 193,600 members; one to every six persons, of whom 81,000 are negroes. The Methodist Episcopal (colored), 13,752; the Methodist Episcopal (North) 12,000 colored, 3000 whites. The African Methodist, 40,000. The colored Presbyterian, 1000. Total *black* membership, 147,700. Total *white* membership, 262,800. Showing of the white population of the State, one church-member to 2.43, and of the blacks, one church-member to 4.02.

THE NEGRO SOCIALLY.

1st. *Has he a liking for labor as labor?*

"There is no fire in his bones impelling him to labor. There is no impulse in his climate or surroundings, no sufficient need, no inherited habits, no illustrations before his eyes. The 'Country Parson' says that even the *whites* could not stand this test; hence, any real love of labor, as such, is either by inheritance or habits founded on the consideration of its fruits. He never seems to feel restless because idle, or to seek work just to be doing something. If his physical wants are supplied, he is perfectly satisfied to do absolutely nothing."

In some of the sea-board counties of Georgia, where fish and game abound, many of the plantations have been abandoned on account of the difficulty in obtaining *continuous labor* in cultivation; the negroes preferring the irregular and indolent habits of the aborigines, and going to labor only when the necessity for clothing compels them to do so.

2d. *Has he a liking for labor as the means to an end?*

"If the reward or inducement be sufficient, he labors very cheerfully; but his satisfaction lies in the result attained, not at all in the fact that it was attained by *his labor.* He would prefer it a *free gift.*"

3d. *What is his character as a laborer?*

"His physical capacity is good. His ability to stand exposure to the sun, miasma, and fever, and to work without exhaustion, are unusual, and instance the survival of the fittest. The wear and tear of his nervous system is small, for he is not eager in his work. If his employment *suits* him, he is very capable and most cheerful. A great deal has been said about the Negro's inferiority to the white man as a laborer, and in many pursuits it is doubtless true, especially so in job-work about towns, where so much depends upon method and economy of time; and also in employments requiring skill and intelligence rather than capacity for physical endurance. But for regular plantation work with the plough, hoe, and axe, the Negro will accomplish as much in a day as any laborer, and will laugh and sing over it; at the close of the day, he has plenty of life left for a coon-hunt or a dance until midnight. He is, however, a routinist, rarely endeavoring to change or improve upon what he has hitherto done, and slow to learn improvements in method from others. Merely muscular labor is his forte. As a laborer, under proper control, he is the best that can be had at present."

4th. *Is he provident?* (Involving the support of his family.)

"He is improvident. Many of them know this. Even if rations are supplied in abundance they will not hold out; much less do they foresee wants and provide for them. He is not provident for his *personal* wants, much less for his family. Apprehension of them is no check to the increase of race."

"Whether this is a natural defect, or the result of slavery, in which state his *owner* was his Providence, and he knew that his family would be provided for, we know not; but, whatever the cause, his improvidence is remarkable. There are, of course, exceptions; but in a majority of instances, when a Negro comes into possession of money, he puts it to immediate use in gratifying any whim for trifling or useless things, and very rarely puts by any for future needs or necessities. His family have always managed to live in the *past,* so his faith wavers not as to the *future.*"

5th. *As a laborer, does he require surveillance?*

"He needs watching; he does not like it, but needs it like a child. He will make constant mistakes in details unless observed, and be very negligent, slighting his work. His judgment is not to be relied on to meet unexpected emergencies."

In this particular it is doubtful if there is much difference between him and the common laborer of the North.

6th. *Is he easily controlled?*

"As a laborer he is very easily controlled, seeming to have an instinctive sense of subordination."

7th. *Is he self-sustaining?* (Away from the encouragement and influence of whites.)

"He is self-sustaining only by the smallness of his wants. He lacks perseverance and energy to work continuously, and cannot resist the temptation to take numerous holidays."

8th. *Has he any desire for education?*

"He is not deficient in the *desire* for education. It is, however, indefinite, and based on love of display and novelty, and an ambition to read and write like 'white folks,' rather than on a love of knowledge. The average of intelligence among them is very low, and is likely to remain so."

9th. *What progress does he make, and what is its limit?*

"In some cases the young Negro is precocious, and will learn the preliminary branches as quickly as the white boy; many have made remarkable progress in branches requiring memory alone; but, as a rule, the desire and capacity both seem to exhaust themselves about the age of (15) fifteen. As a rule, he has better memory than reasoning faculties, yet he improves under cultivation. Sir Samuel Baker compares his first rapid progress to that of one of the inferior animals."

All idea of social or mental equality with the whites is apparently abandoned. Schools are abundantly provided and liberally maintained by the whites; and in the State of Georgia alone 55,000 negro children attended the free schools in 1875. Generally there is no social disorder, and the two races live together in relations of mutual assistance and dependence.

10th. *Has he any social ambition?*

"In towns and cities, from contact with, and in imitation of, the whites, he shows social ambition to some extent. On the plantation there is scarcely a trace of it. The *aristocratic* city Negro copies the white in dress, manners, conversation, and religious worship, and has a great desire to shine. Vanity, not *pride*, is a leading characteristic."

11th. *Is he inclined to, and easily instructed in, mechanical employments?*

"He is decidedly inclined to, and easily instructed in, the coarse and common trades, such as shoemaking, tailoring, blacksmithing, carpentering, joining, rough painting, brick-laying, etc.; and, were he thrifty and forecasting, he could make a living and save money. He rarely becomes a first-class mechanic, and a 'white boss' is generally a necessity."

The Mulatto and Negro differ very decidedly in capacity, mental and physical; the former having the larger mental, and the latter the larger physical development. The greater the proportion of white blood, the greater the mental capacity; and, consequently, the colored men who acquire political prominence, or unusual skill in the trades or the arts, are generally found to be largely indebted to the admixture of white blood. The intermarriage of mulattoes is seldom productive; when it is, the offspring is feeble and sickly, and reared rarely and with great difficulty.

12th. *What is the character of the rising generation?*

"It is thought they are deteriorating in every way; physically, from want of care and proper parental management; mentally and morally, because not controlled as in slavery times. The parents are usually either inert or violent. The comparative worthlessness as laborers of the rising generation is one of the gravest difficulties."

Our opportunities for observing the moral condition of the free plantation laborers have been limited in number, and we hesitate in making any positive statements as to their condition as a whole. But under slavery, the slave, as well as the master, had many advantages. The latter was bound by his personal interests to keep the slave well housed, well clothed, well fed, physically cared for, and decently moral. To the former, these were all blessings which in a state of freedom he is generally denied. In the place of a cleanly white-washed cabin, which he was forced to keep in order, he has a miserable hovel; his clothing is an apology; his food is inferior in quality, and irregular in quantity, or he is without it altogether; his health and sanitary condition he does not understand, and has no care for; his morals are, what might be expected as the natural result of these conditions, generally debased. The planter now naturally considers himself absolved from all consideration or supervision of the mental, moral, or physical condition of his laborer; and, as a consequence, the Negro left to himself and away from all restraining influences, without education or established principles, inherent or acquired, is in a deplorable situation. On some plantations we have visited, adultery, bigamy, and all manner of lewdness exist to a frightful extent without remonstrance from the proprietor. We were present at one time on a plantation where a Negro had committed rape on the person of a young Negro girl, and afterwards compromised with the father by *the promise of a payment of ten dollars!* In the State of South Carolina where the Negro has had control, and notably in the city of Charleston, the older negroes are respectful; but the younger and rising generation, from neglect, bad advice, and the want of proper education, are sullen, wilful, impudent, and excitable, ready and willing at any moment to join in a mob or riot on the slightest provocation. The blacks and whites both commonly carry arms and concealed weapons; and throughout the Southern country, outside the cities and larger towns, the pistol is as much a "*vade mecum*" as a plug of tobacco. Resistance to white domination and control has been openly taught in the church, in the school, and in the political arena, which may account for much that is bad in the present state of the young. There is abundant evidence to show that under slavery, and during the war (as hateful and disorganizing as slavery and war are), the Negro was a better member of society than he is to-day, in his transition state, or, perhaps, ever will be. A reverend gentleman well known in South Carolina, and who now is over a large colored congregation in Charleston, says: "I had during the war the charge of a large parish of over five hundred communicants, on one of the sea islands, where the majority of the population is of the worst class of semi-civilized negroes; and during all that time I never saw or heard of an instance of insulting or impudent conduct on the part of the blacks toward the whites."

But in South Carolina the conditions have been exceptional, and the result is exceptionally injurious to the blacks and whites as well. Totally unfitted by instinct or education for the right of suffrage, or the holding of office, its unreasonable and improvident exercise has been attended by the worst consequences to the State. And the effect of this sudden and conscious inheritance of political power upon the black population, and particularly the rising generation, is as already described.

In Georgia, where latterly the Negro has not been driven to the polls, but allowed to exercise his right or not as he chose, his specific gravity as a political element is somewhat indicated. Under ordinary circumstances he has little interest in, or knowledge of, national or local politics, and he voluntarily denies himself the right to vote; and however paradoxical, unreasonable, or unphilosophical it may appear, the Negro in Georgia, where he has *no* control, is a very much better citizen in every way than he is *now*, or *has* been in South Carolina, where he has had a large share in the government. Education and larger experience may change and improve his present moral and political condition.

13th. *Are the females withdrawing from field labor, and in any sense becoming a burden on the males?*

"The females are very generally withdrawing from field-labor, claiming that their husbands must support them 'like white folks do.' The planters, however, generally demand their labor in any unusual pressure, particularly in cotton picking, as some return for free quarters and fuel during the year. When so employed they are paid wages."

The drift of female labor is towards large centres of population on account of the increased opportunities they afford for social intercourse in the way of religious and society meetings, for satisfying a natural fondness for sights and shows, and for engaging in "*aristocratic*" labor, such as "taking in washing," etc.

14th. *Is insanity frequent?*

"Insanity is now more frequent than formerly in servitude, when it was almost unknown, unless hereditary. In December, 1875, the State lunatic asylum of Georgia had a total of five hundred and eighty-seven patients, of whom ninety were blacks; and the proportion of the latter is thought to be increasing gradually." The rate of mortality, especially in children, has very much increased.

15th. *To what degree does he possess reasoning faculties?*

"As a rule, the Negro reasons imperfectly; his intellectual faculties are weak. His memory, however, is more retentive than his judgment is clear; or, in other words, of the two powers, memory and judgment, the former is the more capable of performing its functions."

THE NEGRO POLITICALLY.

1st. *As an element in politics has he any distinctive character?*

"The *color line* has controlled, and is likely to control. Of the general interests of society he has little conception, and he thinks only in a rude way of his own color. When fully wrought upon by his preacher, or others having influence, and brought into line on a pure *class* and *color* question, he is difficult to move. He is afraid of the vengeance of his own race, and of social ostracism by his fellows.

"Singularly, in all such cases, the women are specially bitter against deserters, being often known to abandon their husbands for voting contrary to their wishes. But unless solidified upon some *class* question, their votes are most easily controlled."

The fear of the loss of their freedom so recently gained, is the great political *lever* by which false and designing men have swayed the colored vote in one coherent, solidified mass for their own base purposes and selfish ends. The United States local officers were supposed to hold the keys to the temple of freedom, and to be able to shut them out, at will.

In blind, childlike confidence did they look up to them, as representing a beneficent government, and as friends upon whom depended the perpetuity of their freedom; to them, they yielded an obedience, simple, absolute, servile.

Has this confidence been betrayed?

Let the depleted and bankrupt treasuries,

The recent anarchical condition of South Carolina,

The depreciation of property and labor,

The abandonment of plantations,

The general stagnation in business,

The insecurity of property,

The increase of taxation,

In short, all the evils disastrous to labor which follow corrupt government, answer.

If the office-holders and others who have brought about this state of things alone suffered, it would be a sufficient compensation; but the Negro voter, remembering the broken promises, his disappointed hopes of Elysian fields, and happy Rasselian valleys where the call to labor never sounds, has lost faith, and is beginning to feel that he has been wronged by his new-found friends, and is again returning slowly, but surely and confidingly, to his former advisers.

2d. *Has he any rank as an element of progress and higher development?*

"None whatever, as a class."

His imitative power is great; but the faculty of origination is wanting. Where the white race leads, he will follow, but always at a distance, in the ratio of their respective capacities.

3d. *What are his qualifications as a voter?*

"At present, except under circumstances described above, the old phrase, 'floating vote,' expresses him as a voter, with a tendency to side against property, intelligence, and virtue; not from opposition to them *as such,* but because of his indistinct conceptions and want of understanding."

From want of opportunity for education, he is of course ignorant, and his negative qualifications may be summed up as follows:—

He neither reads nor writes. He is immoral. He reasons imperfectly. What he is told he remembers confusedly. He has no power of analysis. He is gregarious with his own race. He is easily influenced, but cannot be depended upon, even if he *accepts* a bribe. He has little of what is called "common-sense."

In all these particulars he differs little from the ignorant white voter of the North; but with us at the North the ignorant whites are very greatly in the minority, and the danger and inconvenience in the administration of the government of the smaller towns, arising from their presence, is very slightly felt; while under similar conditions at the South, the Negro is greatly in the *majority*, and the difficulty of managing such a mass of irresponsible voters in the interest of good government is very great, and serious, if by any exciting cause he is brought to the polls. In fact, the *possible* condition of all the Southern cities and towns, with perhaps a few exceptions, is what the *actual* condition of New York is to-day.

4th. *As a factor, in the increase of population, what is his probable future?*

"He is probably a diminishing factor. Under slavery the Southern negroes increased rapidly. Children brought no additional cares. The mother enjoyed certain privileges, immunities, and exemptions, all of which are now wanting; and there was no lack of medical attention or supplies. This state of affairs was guaranteed, not less by humanity than by worldly thrift. Now, another child brings additional expenses, and they prefer *not* to have them. The root of the cotton-plant is known to all Negro women as a powerful emmenagogue, and, being everywhere obtainable, it is extensively used. This is having a decided influence in diminishing natural increase; and the census of 1880 is looked forward to with extreme interest. To this is to be added the further effects of poverty, entailing lack of medical service and medicines, of proper food, clothing, and shelter, and in general the absence of the care taken by their former owners; and the greater prevalence of epidemic diseases caused by their herding together in crowded and filthy quarters in towns and cities. Free from control, dissipation is more frequent and disastrous."

We have not attempted any elaboration of the ideas stated and suggested in the above replies; and have not entered, nor do we propose to enter into any discussion of, or suggestions as to, what *should have been* done with the Negro when he first received his freedom, or to offer any criticism or censure upon what *was* done, or any speculations as to his future. Our object is simply, to the best of our ability, to state the facts of his present condition, obtained from the best sources, and from personal observation.

The correspondent before referred to, sketching his present condition, says: —

"How to help him in his sore need, is rather the province of the philanthropist. To him in the end must we leave the Negro after all. Just now we are regarding him simply as a political factor in the body politic. We have tried him as a legislator, a supreme judge, a major-general, and a policeman. Generally he has been a failure. As a laborer under kind instruction he has often proved a success. And yet, as one sees the hundreds of idle blacks that swarm over the Capitol, lounge in the sun on Pennsylvania Avenue, or crowd the railway-stations and small towns of the South, ill-clad, lazy, worthless, but grinning through their thick lips as if life were all frolic and fun, one cannot help asking the question, whether the intellectual faculties in this race will ever sufficiently predominate over the purely animal instincts to enable them to profit by *any* amount of instruction and advice. Even the severe school of adversity seems to teach them but little. I speak now of the pure Negro, not of the mulatto or quadroon. I envy even the hopefulness of those who believe in any happy future for these poor, ignorant, and despised ones. In God's providence, they doubtless have their purpose. I do not think that their highest function is office-holding or voting. We had no right to suppose they would succeed in this. We have made them the laughing-stock of a whole people. We have brought them to a condition in which they must now stand alone, or fall. To sustain them longer by bayonets is unsafe and impossible. Let us not despair, however. Their removal from politics will at once quiet all opposition to them, and they will go to work to make money and set their little homes in order. This will be a positive gain, both to our politics and business interests.

They begin already to again trust their former masters. Again they seek their advice, and vote with them upon local interests and often upon national ones. The more intelligent of them can already see that when they divide into both parties, they will be sought and flattered by politicians, instead of being 'bulldozed' and murdered. God speed the day when they shall have the courage to vote *any* ticket or *all* tickets, so that it shall become the interest of all parties to consult their interests! Then only will the race taste political freedom. Time and education will slowly help them to rise in the scale of civilization. But the future is sad for them at best. Their young die in large numbers for want of proper nurture, and it must be at best through great tribulation that they finally work out their earthly salvation, and are able to stand alone."

From what has already been stated and suggested, some conclusions as to the capacity of the race for the higher forms of self-government, in its present stage of development may be drawn.

With no correct notions of morals or religion, no accurate conception of the positive duties arising from citizenship, improvident, ignorant, and not self-sustaining, the race is at present entirely unprepared for the responsible duties of freemen; and naturally when the Southern Negro has been called upon to govern he has signally failed.

He is not to blame for this, and is not blamed; his misfortune is understood, and by those who knew him best his failure was foreseen. But notwithstanding this knowledge of his incapacity, the whites, North and South, have, from political or other motives, in many instances recklessly imperilled their own interests, and those of the Negro, by forcing him into positions for which, either by habits or education, he was entirely unfitted.

Many illustrative facts could be given, but one or two will suffice. Hamburg, in the State of South Carolina, is on the Savannah River, and directly opposite to Augusta, Ga. This place was last year the scene of a riot, the particulars of which will be remembered, and in which, in our opinion, the blacks as well as the whites were to blame.

Hamburg was formerly an active, thriving place, with a bank, warehouses, etc., and a good many fortunes were there made, we are told. Before the war, it was the rival of Augusta in cotton-shipping. At its close, it fell into the hands of the black majority, and was fully officered by them. The bank and warehouses are now closed or destroyed, the streets grass-grown and deserted, and its business entirely lost. The city of Charleston, S. C., was also in the hands of the black majority. General stagnation in business followed; money was appropriated, but never spent for the objects for which it was appropriated; the streets were neglected; the sidewalks broken and disordered; the buildings, public and private, in a state of rapid decay and general neglect; and the devastation of war and fire was unrepaired. Improved property was *given away* for ten years, on an obligation to pay the taxes.

If we now turn to Liberia, concerning whose present condition and future prospects, or destiny, scarcely any two observers can agree, we find a government conducted *by* the blacks *for* the blacks, and under which the white man is disfranchised and unrecognized.

Without attempting to settle any disputes, we will try to find a few facts upon which we can all stand.

Looking first at the increase in population. We find that the American Colonization Society in 1820 sent out their first company of eighty-six colonists.

In 1847, when the republic was organized, the Americo-African population was 5,000; aborigines, occupying their territory, 100,000.

In 1856, Americo-African population, 8,000; aborigines, 250,000.

In 1859, the American Colonization Society had sent out to that date 10,000 emigrants at an expense of $1,800,000, of whom only *one-half* were then residents!

In 1873, the Americo-African population was 20,000; aborigines, 700,000, including the two large, powerful, and hostile tribes of Mandingos and Grebos; the former all Mohammedans, and both recently (1876) in a state of insurrection against the Liberian government. It is a remarkable fact that a very large proportion of those emigrants who have been sent out, as well as those who have gone out at their own expense, have returned, and a larger number would have returned if they could. "The colored people are satisfied with their homes here, and resent any measures to remove them."* The earlier colonists have shown a heroism in defence against the savages, as well as in disease and in famine, worthy of any race; and we fear the same heroism will be again demanded in the present generation.

The financial credit of a government or people is a sure indicator of its permanent or temporary condition; and the statement is rather disparaging to Liberia that "a few years ago $500,000 were borrowed in London for 'internal improvements,' which, after deducting two years' interest, paid in advance, agents' commissions, etc., netted to Liberia $200,000 *in gold and useless goods,* which soon disappeared *without an internal* improvement."†

Her inability to pay either principal or interest is now apparent, and unfortunately "she lies at the mercy of her bondholders."‡

In agriculture very little progress has been made. Horses, mules, and asses cannot endure the climate, and soon die: the very luxuriance of vegetation increasing the difficulty and labor in the growth of crops. But very few manufactures have been established.

In 1857, thirty-seven years after the arrival of the first colonists, with a population of 8,000 Americo-Africans, her schools and churches were supported by American Christians, and to-day there is very little, if any, interest in higher education, or the support of common schools! The experience of Liberia is that of the South, as before stated. The desire and capacity of the Negro for education seem to ex-

* Paper read at the Sixtieth Annual Meeting of American Colonization Society by E. P. Humphrey, D.D., LL.D.

† Commodore Shufeldt's Address before American Colonization Society, Jan. 18, 1876.

‡ Commodore Shufeldt.

haust themselves at an early age. "I regret to say that a college has been lately established in Liberia. . . . I regret it, because it will involve an outlay that might be better used in common schools. . . . The present state of society in Liberia has no demand for such a thing."*

The climate and surroundings, the abundance of natural products of the soil to be obtained without labor, the absence of the necessity for clothing or habitations, except of the rudest sort, render the Americo-African, as well as the aborigines, indolent, indifferent, improvident; and any natural impulse for higher development is entirely wanting. If the impulse is implanted, and left to itself to increase and multiply, without constant encouragement and assistance from a superior race, it will soon exhaust itself. Archbishop Whately says: "We have no reason to believe that any community ever did, or ever can, emerge, unassisted by external helps, from a state of utter barbarism into anything that can be called civilization."†

"It is evident that physical geography has blighted Africa with the curse of barbarism,"‡ and if she is ever to be Christianized and civilized, as we hope in the providence of God she may, it will only be accomplished by the blacks, as humble instruments in the hands of a superior race. All travellers agree that Mohammedanism is spreading over Africa with marvellous strides, and the work of evangelization accomplished will of course be in proportion to the means used. But progress must of necessity be slow, "and with regard to education and civilization we must be satisfied to work gradually, and not to attempt to force our European manners and customs upon a people who are at present unfitted for them."§ Referring to the results of colonization in Africa, Chaplain Thomas remarks: "We would not be understood as attributing any unworthy motive to the zealous friends of the Americo-African in Liberia; they are noble

*** Rev. C. W. Thomas, M.A., "West Coast of Africa."**

† "Political Economy," p. 68. **‡ Bowen's "Central Africa."**

§ Com. Cameron, "Across Africa."

and liberal men. But we wish to intimate, that, in looking at and describing the condition of their long-cherished scheme, their desires too often color their statements."*

It must be admitted that the picture we have drawn of the Negro, as a *race*, is not a flattering one; and we wish that in some particulars it was not a true one. But we have for him no word of reproach; there is room for nothing but pity. When he received his freedom he was a child in intellect, in education, in dependence, in simplicity; and he has become what children with coarse animal instincts usually become without proper training. The Negro character, however, has its lights as well as shadows.

There *are* pious and godly men and women; good husbands and devoted wives; fond and loving and careful parents; devoted and sacrificing friends; honest and upright citizens. As a laborer, he is willing, cheerful, and of great physical capacity; insensible to exposure, miasma, and fever; easily controlled, and is altogether the best that can be had.

In the States where they have not of late years been forced into the political arena, the blacks are quiet and unobtrusive, attending, in large centres, to all the duties of life to the limit of their capacity, in the same manner as the whites in the same condition of life. In the State of Georgia they are credited as owning $8,000,000 in property. The schools for colored people are well patronized, and the number attending school very large and rapidly increasing. A gentleman in Augusta, Ga., tells us he has sold over two hundred house-lots to colored people, who have paid for them in small instalments since the war. The more thrifty in towns own a mule and cultivate their little lots about their houses, and engage in all sorts of employment adapted to their capacities, dress like "white folks," and go to meeting on Sundays.

In the country, they own, or lease and cultivate, small farms of one hundred acres or more, paying the rent in the product. A Southern gentleman, formerly a large slave-owner, tells us of one who has been his tenant for several

* Rev. C. W. Thomas, M.A., "West Coast of Africa."

years, and describes him as being, in all his dealings with him, prompt, courteous, careful, and, by instinct, a perfect gentleman.

As a rule, however, we fear that they are not successful as proprietors. The country Negro does not pay the attention to dress which his city brother does; but always goes to "meeting," if one is held within walking distance.

The wages paid on large plantations are very small compared with our Northern rate. The able-bodied men get $8.00 per month and found in rations of one-half pound of bacon and two pounds of meal daily, for each full hand, besides rent of cabin. The women get $4.00, $5.00, and $6.00, according to working ability, with rations. The daily rations are valued at ten cents, and are served only to the *laborer*, and not to his or her family.

Tobacco is used by men and women alike. By the courtesy of a large Southern planter who allowed us the use of his books of account, we were able to make some curious memoranda as to the domestic habits of the Negro. And among them in the use of tobacco, we found that the foreman of the mill, a superior hand, who was paid $10.00 per month, spent $3.30 in the weed. Some who were paid $8.00 per month spent, respectively, $2.15, $1.65, .80, $1.20, $1.00, and $2.00 in a month. An engineer who received $15.00, spent $4.35 in tobacco. A woman who was paid $4.00 wages, spent $1.65. In fancy goods for the women, such as highly-colored hats, dresses, parasols, and fancy high-heeled shoes, etc., and for the men, fine hats, fancy stockings (which, with the shoes, they take off and carry in their hands to the vicinity of the meeting-house), candies, canned lobsters and peaches, cigars, etc., etc., some of the hands spent, respectively, $1.90, .62, $1.00, .55, $2.00, .84, $1.75, .70 during the month. The average amount spent monthly for tobacco, by men and women, was $2.00 each: for luxuries, etc., $1.17 each. Total, $3.17, or 35 per cent. of the average wages. The average wages for men and women are $9.10 per month; deducting the amount spent as above, we have a balance of $5.93 left to each hand monthly, for the support of his young children, and, frequently, the wife, in food, clothing, and the usual necessaries of existence. For an average family of five non-working members, it would afford to each one the pittance of twenty cents daily. It is not much to be wondered at that he is frequently driven to rob a hen-roost, or shoot a stray pig, to satisfy the cravings of a hungry family.

The question is often asked, "Is there any antagonism of races in the South?" Under the usual normal conditions, there is not. In South Carolina, where, as we have before stated, antagonism has been encouraged in the negroes, and in Mississippi, Arkansas, and Louisiana, where they have been unduly excited in a variety of ways, and openly taught that the object and purpose of the whites was to *re-enslave* them — which result would follow immediately upon the success of the Democratic party, — there has, undoubtedly, been bad feeling; and excesses and crimes have been committed by whites and blacks, and probably a greater number by the whites than by the blacks,—as when the former are attacked or seek revenge, their means and opportunities are greater and more numerous. But for this great change in the disposition of a race once proverbially docile, obedient, and law-abiding, and now intractable, impudent, and dangerous, there must of necessity be an adequate exciting cause. The Southern people understand the Negro well, and they know that this unnatural lawlessness is *foreign* to the race; that it is not innate in them, and does not proceed, generally, from any injury or oppression undergone or experienced; but is the offspring of an over-heated imagination and very excitable temperament, wrought upon by outside agencies for the accomplishment of political results. Consequently, as far as our observation extends, we have yet to find any evidence of the existence of indignity or bitterness on the part of the whites towards the blacks, excepting, of course, those cases in which the life and property of inoffensive persons have by the latter been wilfully destroyed; but, on the contrary, we have found pity for the colored people, and contempt and disgust for their unprincipled leaders, everywhere expressed. This sympathy for the Negro is, in many cases, active and practical. We know of many Southern gentlemen who now support whole families of their old slaves and descendants, numbering ten or twelve each, not having the heart to turn them out upon the world; and yet, strange to say, these same negroes, submitting to other control, will vote against what their old masters suppose to be their interest in the support of honest government, and still return to the paternal roof-tree to be supported and protected as formerly.

We at the North understand very little, and it is, in fact, impossible for us to fully comprehend the love and affection which the Southern people have for their old nurses and house-servants; and there are many instances of the former having separate establishments and comfortable homes provided for their declining years as a reward for faithful service, in which they are cared for and supported with tenderness and solicitude. We personally know of heads of families who, since the war and the misfortune following, have deprived their own children of certain rather expensive necessaries and luxuries in order to bestow them on some faithful old servant. There are other instances in which the loss of fortune, and consequent poverty, are mutually and inseparably borne by master, mistress, and servant alike,—literally "bearing one another's burdens." To the credit of the colored people, be it said, that this extreme kindness and affection are frequently reciprocated; and during the war when distress, misfortune, and want were everywhere felt, the faithful blacks were able in many ways, impossible to their masters or mistresses, to relieve distress, furnish comfort in misfortune, and supply physical wants.

W. Lawrence, in his "Natural History of Man," speaking of the whole race, says: "Many of them, although little civilized, display an openness of heart, a friendly and generous disposition, the greatest hospitality, and an observance of the point of honor, according to their own notions, from which nations more advanced in knowledge might often take a lesson with advantage."

When their freedom was first declared, it was followed by a general desertion and changing of masters, sometimes very abruptly and unpleasantly; but it was usually borne by the whites with composure, understanding, as they did, that it was the only method known to the blacks by which they could *test* their freedom, and ascertain its actual existence. But the older servants gradually returned to their old homes, and to their former occupations. These separations of master and servant were frequently more painful to the former than the latter. We have seen the eyes of an old mistress fill with tears as she told us of the going away of a favorite servant, in a manner which appeared to her unfeeling.

The repugnance to colored people universal at the North, among all classes and shades of political opinion, however we may attempt its concealment, from party or other motives, has no existence at the South. Suckled and fondled in infancy, petted and indulged in childhood, and revered by them in later years, the Southern people still feel for them a kindliness and sympathy by us unfelt and unrecognized.

We will not attempt to discuss the problem of the Southern Negro's future in this country; but there are a few thoughts naturally suggested by what has gone before, which we will briefly state.

It is evident that from climatic and other influences, and consequent low mental capacity, no *comparison* can properly lie between the black and white races. It is said that "no European people has been in a condition comparable to that of the present dark-colored races, within the reach of any history or tradition."* It is evident that the black is, and will continue to be, a *dependent race.* It is evident that, owing to natural repugnance, there is no hope for them in amalgamation with the white race. It is one of the possibilities, but not one of the probabilities, of the future.

It is evident that the dissolution of our philanthropic societies at the close of the war was a *very grave error.* That, although the prominent object of the anti-slavery

* W. Lawrence, "Natural History of Man."

societies was accomplished by devastation and war, the opportunity for the exercise of true philanthropy and an enlarged Christian charity was then, as never before, presented. That, owing to this neglect, the colored population of the South have lost moral ground which will never be recovered. It may be said, and is said, that the South must take care of its own population. Undoubtedly they have the disposition, and generally do what they can, to aid them, by furnishing means for education, etc.; but they have not the means to do much, and in the hurry and anxiety incident to getting a living, and in replacing the old, or building up a new fortune, the social and moral condition of the black man is neglected or overlooked. Christian men and women, North and South, may well ask why the solicitude and Christian charity so universal for the colored man before his freedom, without any particular thought of the obligation of his master, should now be partially withdrawn, or cease altogether, when charity has a free course, and the negro stands before us armed with freedom, and clothed with all the rights of a freeman, but, as we have seen, totally unprepared for his duties as such, and sorely in need of the helping hand and outstretched arm of the philanthropic Christian, for guidance and support in his hour of trial.

It is evident that we can best help him by recognizing his actual condition and capacities; that we cannot expect great progress or high culture, and that his interests and our own, as common citizens, will be best promoted by abandoning the forcing process, either in education or politics.

It is evident that the halo of false sentiment and poetic fiction which naturally surrounds an object distant and obscure, is a serious injury to the Negro, in causing demands to be made upon him, and upon those among whom his lot is cast, which neither he nor they are able to meet, and thus contributing to the misunderstanding, which, owing to mistakes as to facts, too much prevails.

It is evident that colonization has a feeble hold upon the Southern Negro. He prefers the support, assistance, and sympathy of the white race. In fact, he is our *ward in honor,* and we are bound by humanity, by the credit of a superior civilization and race, by the oppression and injustice he has already suffered at our hands, to raise him, by education, to a higher plane than he now occupies, and to fit him for the exercise of his civil rights.

It is evident that his rights, political and social, are in no jeopardy at the South, so long as he does not lend himself to foreign politicians to be used as a tool in carrying out their designs, subversive of good government and good morals and against common property.

In conclusion, we commend the thoughtful consideration of this subject and the facts presented, to those who, under the new administration of Southern affairs, honestly desire a better, a more accurate and just knowledge of the present condition, value, and capabilities of that race, now endowed with the highest honors and privileges of American citizenship.

www.ingramcontent.com/pod-product-compliance
Lightning Source LLC
LaVergne TN
LVHW021201120826
845150LV00011B/2339